MW00777072

Anger:
Aim It in the Right Direction

Joni Eareckson Tada

ROSE PUBLISHING/ASPIRE PRESS

Torrance, California

Anger: Aim It in the Right Direction
© Copyright 2015 Joni Eareckson Tada

Aspire Press, an imprint
of Rose Publishing, Inc.
4733 Torrance Blvd., #259
Torrance, California 90503 USA
www.rose-publishing.com
www.aspirepress.com

Printed by Regent Publishing Services Ltd.
Printed in China
November 2014, 1st printing

Contents

The Author

Joni Eareckson Tada, the founder and chief executive officer of Joni and Friends International Disability Center, is an international advocate for people with disabilities. A diving accident in 1967 left Joni Eareckson, then 17,  a quadriplegic in a wheelchair. After two years of rehabilitation, she emerged with new skills and a fresh determination to help others in similar situations. She founded Joni and Friends in 1979 to provide Christ-centered programs to special needs families, as well as training to churches. Through the organization's *Christian Institute on Disability*, Joni and her team have helped develop disability ministry courses of study in major Christian universities and seminaries. Visit us at www.joniandfriends.org.

Are You Angry at God?

Leslie (not her real name) learned recently that her husband Ray was seeing another woman. She was stunned. When Ray told his wife that he had decided to stay with the other woman, it shattered Leslie's life. At first her shock and anger was directed against her husband: *How can he throw away our marriage? How will I support myself?* But as time wore on, another list of angry questions surfaced: *Lord, is this what you do to your people who trust you? Why have you abandoned me and the kids to face this awful nightmare?*

Leslie was becoming angry at God and she knew it. *Am I supposed to paste on a good Christian smile and pretend everything's okay? I can't relate to the Bible anymore when it tells me to not complain.*

Perhaps you've been there. Maybe your boss fired you unfairly, or you were abused as a child. Perhaps you've been betrayed or you're dealing with a progressive disease. Maybe your *child* is dealing with the disease and you are *angry* at God. You tense up when you think of him being sovereign over your life and all its misery.

As "natural" as anger may be, it has incredible potential to destroy. Some describe it as a black energy that demands immediate release and relief. Ironically, this sort of anger—unrighteous anger—ends up turning on us. It lies to us, telling us that if we would just explode and let off a little steam, we'd be okay. But when we do, we're left feeling empty and despairing.

What Is Anger?

What is anger? Many dictionaries describe it as an intense emotional state induced by displeasure. But this definition is too vague. It's one thing to feel displeasure over a car breakdown or rain on our picnic. But when we get angry at a person, we are displeased with a choice she made or an act he performed. Anger at a person always implies strong disapproval. If you are angry at me, you think I have done something I should not have done.

The *emotion* of anger: Anger is a natural emotion—but anger is a secondary feeling. That is, it's suggestive of something deeper: either we've been wronged and wounded emotionally or our sense of rights has been violated (I have the right to be understood, to be treated fairly, etc.). Ephesians 4:26–27 shows not only that the feelings of anger are likely but that they must be dealt with: "'In your anger do not sin': Do not let the sun go down while you are still angry, and do not give the devil a foothold."

The *action* of anger: The Bible underscores that anger itself is not sinful; it's what we do with anger or how we express it that often gets us into trouble. Psalm 4:4 says, "In your anger do not sin; when you are on your beds, search your hearts and be silent."

When does anger lead us to sin?

Everyday Anger

Even the daily frustrations and irritations of life can help us grow if we "aim them at God." To understand what I mean, consider this typical example from my life.

How does anger start?

The other day I had to drive down the 101 Freeway to make an 11:00 a.m. appointment in Burbank. I thought I had given myself plenty of time, but you know Los Angeles traffic. Tension was beginning to rise and I felt frustrated at my friend who was inching along 20 yards behind the vehicle in front of us. "Can't you go faster?!" I tried not to sound harsh, but we both knew anger was in my words.

What is anger telling you?

Consider my problem on the 101 Freeway: Pride was involved because I was ashamed of showing up late… selfishness was involved because I was discontent with the way my friend was driving… mistrust was at the root of it all, for I felt as though God had forgotten us in the traffic.

What is factual about your situation?

Basically, I needed to trust that God was in control—of the time, the traffic, and my friend driving. God was more interested in confronting my pride and selfishness, rather than my punctuality.

Can you confess anger and ask God for help?

God often allows irritating situations in our lives to teach us lessons about himself as well as about us. God uses irritating situations like bad traffic, broken washing machines, missed appointments, or bounced checks to force you and me to examine our hearts, confess wrong responses, and then draw closer to Christ. This is the way to deal constructively with anger.

Anger Aimed in the Wrong Direction

You see, all of our emotions are corrupted by sin. We need to bring our anger and hurt—and all the rest of our emotions—into the transforming presence of God. If we fail to submit our anger to God, that anger leads us away from God—that's "unrighteous anger." It allows strong feelings of displeasure against God and his choices or actions in our life to foment and fester. Unrighteous anger breeds mistrust of God and eventually loathes dependence on God. The sad thing about this kind of anger is that it sucks the last vestige of hope from our hearts. We stop caring and feeling. We commit a silent suicide of the soul, allowing despair to move in like a damp fog, deadening our heart to the hope that we will ever be happy again.

John Piper explains, "It is wrong—always wrong—to disapprove of God for what he does and permits. 'Shall not the Judge of all the earth do what is just?' (Gen. 18:25). It is arrogant for finite, sinful creatures to disapprove of God for what he does and permits. We may weep over the pain. We may be angry at sin and Satan. But God does only what is right. 'Yes, O Lord God, the Almighty, true and righteous are Your judgments' (Rev. 16:7)."

When Anger Turns to Despair: A Personal Story

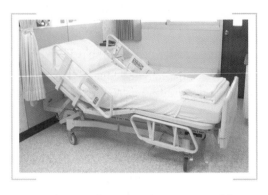

Somewhere after the first year of lying paralyzed in my hospital bed, somewhere after my bleak prognosis of a lifetime of total paralysis drained every ounce of hope—even anger, both righteous and unrighteous—out of me, despair moved in. I refused to get up for physical therapy. I turned my head away when friends came to visit. I felt numb and emotionless (a clear symptom of anger that turns to despair). I didn't even have anything to say to the nurses and hospital aids that had become friends.

Hazel was a nurse's aide from Mississippi who noticed I was slipping away. She knew I had taken a liking to her. She would amble into my room, pull up a chair, and take her breaks by my bedside. "Wanna tell me about it, girl?" she'd ask, lighting up her cigarette. I gave her no reply. I just stared straight ahead. Hazel would smile, slowly blowing smoke in the other direction. I'd grunt. "You feel like bawling, you just tell me. I've got a kerchief here handy," she'd say, patting her pocket. "Um." I didn't want to talk.

I was so despairing, I didn't even want to eat. Once when Hazel was feeding me dinner, half-chewed food dribbled out of the side of my mouth. "What in the world are you doing?!" she shouted. My body reacted with a violent spasm. Hazel slammed down the plate of food and peas scattered everywhere. She forcefully wiped my mouth, crumpled the napkin, and threw it on the tray. "You get yourself together, girl. Ain't nothing wrong with you that a good look around this hospital won't cure." My cheeks flushed with embarrassment. I fought back tears. "Now are you gonna eat this or what?!"

Hazel had roused deep feelings of resentment. "Yes," I spat back, "I'll eat it!" The food was tasteless, and I forced myself to swallow against a knotted stomach. Not a word was spoken between us. After she left, I struggled harder to contain the tears. I could not allow myself to cry because there would be no one to blow my nose or change my damp pillow.

Suddenly I realized, *I'm feeling something.* Like a hibernating animal waking up, I felt something stir. The numb emotions were dissipating and in their place, there was a magnetic pull toward hope. That night, I found myself saying out loud, "God, if I can't die, please show me how to live." It was short, to the point, but it left the door open for him to respond. Little did I realize he would: "The Lord is close to the brokenhearted and saves those who are crushed in spirit" (Ps. 34:18).

Thank God that, in his mercy, he moved in my heart that way. I thank him that he refused to permit my puny shield of unrighteous anger to stall him. Thankfully, he was intolerant of my despair, and so he encroached, presumed, invaded, and infringed on my thoughts. He tore aside the curtains of my despondency and threw open doors I had locked around my heart. He hit the light switch in my dark soul and pierced my complacency. He boldly intruded into my self-pity, brashly calling it what it was and challenging me to leave it behind.

Anger Aimed in the *Right* Direction

The biblical way to handle anger is to be transparent before the Lord, *while at the same time not blaspheme or badmouth him, turn your back on him, or sow seeds of discord about him.* Rather than say things you'll only regret later on, *learn how to complain in a godly way!*

There is such a thing as "holy lamenting," my friend David Powlison says. In God's Word you can find the lamentations of other people who felt cheated and forgotten by God. Borrow their language. Let their psalms and lamentations give voice to your pain. Don't move away from God… move toward him. Don't turn your back on God… face him. It's the biblical and constructive way to resolve your anger.

The Psalms: A Place of Anger and Hope

Over the following weeks, I sensed a stronger interest in the Bible. When I lay face down on the Stryker frame, I was able to flip the pages of a Bible with my mouth stick. I didn't know where to turn, but the psalms intrigued me. I found an amazing Psalm whose words perfectly matched what I had been going through…

O LORD, the God who saves me,
day and night I cry out before you.
May my prayer come before you;
turn your ear to my cry.
For my soul is full of trouble
and my life draws near the grave.
I am counted among those who go
down to the pit;
I am like a man without strength.
I am set apart with the dead,
like the slain who lie in the grave,
whom you remember no more,
who are cut off from your care.

—Psalm 88:1–5

I was fascinated that there was a psalm with which I could totally identify—*oh my, the Bible understands me! God understands exactly how I feel.* As more time passed, I was not so much interested in the despair of Psalm 88, but in the other 149 psalms which hinted more of hope.

Will the Lord reject us forever?
Will he never show his
favor again?
Has his unfailing love
vanished forever?
Has his promise failed for all time?
Has God forgotten to be merciful?
Has he in anger withheld his
compassion?

—Psalm 77:7–9

Just look at Psalm 77! Six rapid-fire questions packed with explosive power. The psalmist's despair turns godly when it turns godward. Something awesome has to happen when we choose the direct line to the Lord. "The irony of questioning God is that it honors him: it turns our hearts away from ungodly despair toward a passionate desire to comprehend him," says Dr. Dan Allender. The psalmist's questions serve as a reality check, exposing any fantasy we hold of a blissful world with no problems.

Lastly, these six questions are not just penned by a sobbing psalmist; these utterances are the Word of God. Something suffering-shaking happens when we hand-pick a psalm to voice our heart-wrenching questions: "For the word of God is living and active" (Heb. 4:12). We are speaking God's language, echoing his own words back to him. When

we wrap our anguish around a biblical psalm,
we're searching for him. And when we seek,
we will find.

Despair Turned Godward

Gut-wrenching questions honor God. Despair directed at God is a way of encountering him, opening ourselves up to the One and only Someone who can actually do something about our plight. And whether we collide with the Almighty or simply bump up against him, we cannot be the same. We never are when we experience God.

The damp fog of my despair did not dissipate overnight, but I knew beyond a shadow of a doubt I had turned a corner. I was moving in the direction of God. My questions also created a paradox: In the midst of God's absence, I felt his presence. I found him after I let go of what I thought he should be. My despair ended up being my ally, because through it, he took hold of me.

Our questions don't always get answers. No cure has been discovered for cancer, countries are still warring against one another, and drunk drivers are still on the road. No wonder we ask God "Why?!" often with a clenched fist. But understanding God's answers doesn't always dissipate our frustration. Sometimes when we cry out to God in anger and frustration, the main relief is simply knowing God is there.

My friend, Jim, knows all about this. He often has to leave his three little boys when he flies away on business. On a recent trip, as the family drove together to the airport, the seven-year-old gladly took last-minute instructions on "how to help Mommy" while Daddy was away. The five-year-old bravely tucked in his chin and promised he would do his chores. As they turned into the airport, the two-year-old, all smiles up until then, spotted an airplane on the runway. Suddenly, he was wailing and sobbing!

"It tore my heart out," Jim told me, "I almost canceled the trip right then. I just kept hugging that little boy." As I saw his eyes well up with tears, I thought, *If that boy's cries tug at Jim's heart, how much more must our tears move our heavenly Father.* Nothing grips God's heart like the tortured cry of one of his children.

Watch what takes place in Psalm 18 after David says, "I cried to my God for help." God is roused.

> From his temple he heard my voice;
> my cry came before him, into his
> ears.
> The earth trembled and quaked,
> and the foundations of the
> mountains shook...
> he parted the heavens and
> came down...
> he mounted the cherubim and flew;
> he soared on the wings of the
> wind...
> he reached down...
> and took hold of me.
>
> —Psalm 18:6–7, 9–10, 16

Our cries powerfully move the Almighty. He parts heaven and shakes earth to respond. He reaches down and takes hold. Jesus is God's way of taking hold of us. When it comes to heartfelt questions and despair, Jesus experienced both like no human ever has. He did not linger in the damp fog of Gethsemane, succumbing to despair. He moved in the direction of his Father and proceeded to the cross. There, he aimed his cries godward, not choosing his own words to wrap around his wretchedness, but—you guessed it—the words of a psalm. "My God, my God, why have you forsaken me?" he groaned, quoting Psalm 22:1. As our representative, it was not only his cry, but the cry of all humanity. The words are full of pathos and prophecy, a lament that foreshadows the suffering of us all.

But it doesn't stop there. Can God the Father turn a deaf ear to the plea of his own Son? The answer resounds from an empty tomb three days later: *No, may it never be!* And because the Father raised Jesus from the dead, there is hope for us all. "My God, why have you forsaken me," was the cry of Christ on behalf of all humanity, so that in contrast, he could tenderly say to us, "Never will I forsake you" (Heb. 13:5).

Despair which rises in a direct and vertical line to God opens us up to change, real hope and the possibility of seeing God as he really is, not as we want him to be. Once we give an inch, God will take a mile. He'll take a million miles. Today, take your anger and hurt to the Lord. When you do, he'll reach down to embrace you and give you new and fresh hope!

A Personal Story, Part 2

When I was first injured, I felt devastated by total paralysis—the idea of never using my hands or walking overwhelmed me with grief, despair, and hopelessness. Years later after I released my anger and began trusting God, I started having chronic pain. I couldn't help but think, *God, do you know what you're doing?!* Then a few years ago, I received the diagnosis of stage three breast cancer. I felt fearful of the future as I faced getting older in my wheelchair, and I struggled with anger when God piled on *more* problems on top of my quadriplegia. Like, *Hello, God? What are you thinking here?* Let me tell you what I did when I was tempted to angrily blame God for dealing too harshly with me.

1. As soon as doubts, fears, and anger started to encroach (and it always seemed to creep up on me in the middle of the night); when doubts started to choke out my confidence in God, I quickly turned it around and reaffirmed my belief in God's care and provision in my life. I remembered his wisdom and goodness toward me when times were easier. And I remembered these things *quickly*. I did not want to give the Enemy a foothold. Instead, I thought, *God is good; he has my best interests at heart; he is kind and merciful, and he doesn't take his hands off the wheel of my life for a nanosecond. He's in control, and he's got reasons for allowing all this.*

Resist the demand to know God's secret things, and learn to rest in God's revealed things.

2. I rejected the temptation to accuse God of plotting evil in my life. Although many so-called Christian counselors tell people that it's okay to vent your anger against God in a full-force, no-holds-barred way; although they say you need to "forgive God," it's *wrong* advice.

- Complain to God as the psalmist did, but never cast a dark shadow on God's good name.

- Bring your questions before God, but never talk behind his back, spreading poisonous accusations about his character.

- Express your thoughts to Christian friends with whom you're intimate, but never sow seeds of discord about him among others, ruining their faith.

- Invite Christian friends to help you wrestle through your feelings, but never try to get people "on your side" against God.

3. I recognized my limited ability to understand God's ways. I realize I have a finite and fallen mind that is incapable of comprehending God's dealings with people. I had to recognize I'm not responsible for figuring out God's plan—only for knowing, trusting, and pleasing him. Someone wisely said, "Resist the demand to know God's secret things, and learn to rest in God's revealed things." That's great advice.

4. I discovered a more accurate focus for my anger. Satan. Satan was the one who started this whole mess. Disease and death, deformities and catastrophes of nature. He was the one who, because of pride, brought on himself—and us—every horror of the curse.

I implore you today to make the Psalms one of your favorite places to turn to in God's Word. Let the Psalms be an expression—a prayer even—for your heartache and hurt. Allow the comfort and encouragement of the Psalms to wash over you and get you moving in the right direction toward the Lord Jesus. Do it today… and you'll discover the purpose for not only your anger, but also for every emotion.

"Pondering the character of God does not pacify anger; it deepens it. Our struggle is never that we are too angry, but that we are never angry enough. Our anger is always pitifully small when it is focused against a person or object; it is meant to be turned against all evil and all sin."

Dr. Dan Allender and
Dr. Tremper Longman III,
The Cry of the Soul

Turn Your Anger Against the Real Enemy

Anger like this gave birth to Mothers Against Drunk Driving. Help For Victims of Violent Crimes. Just Say No. Child Help. Battered Wives Anonymous. These are just a sampling of how people used their anger to inspire entire movements which have pushed back darkness and brought light and awareness to our society.

I'll never forget several years ago visiting Auschwitz and Birkenau, the dreadful Nazi death camps of World War II where millions of Jews, Poles, and others were exterminated. I sat by the train station where men, women, and children, crammed into box cars, were emptied out onto the ice and dirt to face growling dogs and guards. Children were gun-butted one way, their mothers herded the other. Men were separated into groups of the old and the young. But virtually all of them ended up in one place—the incinerator that was crumbled and overgrown at the far end of the railroad tracks.

My husband picked up a piece of rusted barbed wire. We stared at it, quietly considering the horror and evil which fueled the gas chambers. When we lowered our heads to pray, all I could think of was my disgust for the Devil and his hordes.

Do I not hate those
who hate you, O LORD,
and abhor those who rise up
against you?
I have nothing but hatred for them;
I count them my enemies.

—**Psalm 139:21–22**

An Answer for Anger

And, friend, if you are struggling with feelings of anger toward the Lord because of what seems to be unjust or unfair circumstances… if you feel cheated or forgotten, then I want to encourage you today to move toward God, not away from him.

The Psalms show the heart not only how to speak but to listen. If emotions are the language of the soul, then the book of Psalms gives us the grammar and syntax, teaching us how to wrestle, inviting us to rage, question, and vent anger in such a way as to move up and out of despair. The Psalms wrap nouns and verbs around our pain better than any other book.

Long enough, God—
you've ignored me long enough.
I've looked at the back
of your head
long enough. Long enough
I've carried this ton of trouble,
lived with a stomach full of pain.
Long enough my arrogant enemies
have looked down their noses at me.

—Psalm 13:1–2, *The Message*

The Psalms tell us what to do with our anger. The prescription is succinctly written in Psalm 37:7–8, 11.

> Be still before the LORD and wait patiently for him... refrain from anger and turn from wrath; do not fret—it leads only to evil... [those who lack anger] will inherit the land and enjoy great peace.

Merely replacing a destructive feeling by pasting on a smile is a surface solution, like white washing greasy walls or putting Band-Aids over gaping wounds. A deeper transformation is needed. And so God asks us to wait.

> In your anger do not sin; when you are on your beds, search your hearts and be silent.
>
> —Psalm 4:4

Good advice! The old Puritans had a word for it: "Sit with yourself," they would say. Or, sit with your rage. Waiting is not denial nor is it a distraction. It is refraining from evil, turning from wrath, counting to ten, as it were, to let the steam escape. It is not "doing nothing"; it is a definitive and spiritual exercise. Choosing to wait on God takes you beyond the immediate problems, the painful circumstances, and catapults you, without delay, into the presence of the Lord.

> I am still confident of this:
> I will see the goodness of the LORD
> in the land of the living.
> Wait for the LORD;
> be strong and take heart
> and wait for the LORD.

—Psalm 27:13–14

Did you read that promise? We can be confident that while we are still alive and kicking and in the midst of deep suffering, we *will see* the goodness of the Lord. Awesome!

Books by Joni Eareckson Tada

The topics of fear and hopelessness, depression and suffering, loneliness and worry are issues that author Joni Eareckson Tada can speak to personally. Let Joni tell you her secrets to peace and joy. She knows that God does not take pleasure in seeing you suffer. He has compassion for you and gives you many ways to deal with life's pain so that you can have peace.

Anger: Aim it in the Right Direction

We all have times of anger, disappointment, and frustration. Joni reveals her own struggle with anger after hearing the news that she would never walk again. Find out what she learned from the Bible about how to deal with anger—and get practical tips on how to deal with deep-rooted frustration.

Paperback, 4"x 6", 48 pages,
ISBN 9781628621587

Breaking the Bonds of Fear

Is fear causing you to lose sleep, stress out, and worry? When Joni Eareckson Tada experienced a tragic accident that left her quadriplegic, fear gripped her life. Joni explains the steps she took—and still takes daily—to grow in confidence in the Lord and break the bonds of fear.

Paperback, 4"x 6", 48 pages, ISBN 9781628620481

Gaining a Hopeful Spirit

Finding hope in a tough situation is often easier said than done. But you can experience hope and peace again as you deepen your understanding of who God is. Discover how to place God as the anchor of your life, and find out how to recognize the lies of the enemy that try to prevent you from living a life full of joy and worship.

Paperback, 4"x 6", 48 pages, ISBN 9781628621594

God's Hand in Our Hardship

When you read through the Bible, you can see that God hates suffering. So why doesn't our all-powerful God get rid of suffering? Joni Eareckson Tada tackles the big questions about suffering: How can a gracious and loving God allow anyone to suffer? Why do "good" people have to suffer? What possible good can come through suffering?

Paperback, 4"x 6", 48 pages, ISBN 9781628620474

Making Sense of Suffering

When you're overwhelmed by pain and problems, it's easy to feel helpless, hopeless, and sinking into a whirlpool of self-pity. Joni Eareckson Tada knows about these emotions first hand. Joni shares biblical insights that bring hope and comfort to those who are trying to make sense of their suffering.

Paperback, 4"x 6", 48 pages, ISBN 9781628620467

Prayer: Speaking God's Language

How can we draw closer to God in prayer?
How can we "speak God's language"? As
Christians grow in the discipline of praying,
it becomes clear that there is always more to
learn. Joni Eareckson Tada shares personal
stories and insights that will help you hone
your skill of praying with the Word of God.

Paperback, 4"x 6", 48 pages,
ISBN 9781628620498

A Thankful Heart in a World of Hurt

You already know that you have so much
to be thankful for, but sometimes it's hard
to feel thankful. After living in a wheelchair
for over 45 years, Joni Eareckson Tada
understands. Weaving together practical
insight and Scripture, she tackles key
question, such as: How can I really give
thanks for all things? and Why should I?

Paperback, 4"x 6", 48 pages, ISBN 9781628621563

Where's My Miracle?

You know that God answers prayers, but what
do you do when your situation isn't changing?
Joni shows you the right way and the wrong
way of coming to the Lord for healing and
reveals what the Bible says (and doesn't say)
about healing. Find out how to live a life of
joy (not anxiety) as you wait upon the Lord.

Paperback, 4"x 6", 48 pages, ISBN 9781628621570